OVERCOMING

MARIJUANA ABUSE

BRIDEY HEING

Rosen
YA
™
New York

Published in 2019 by The Rosen Publishing Group, Inc.
29 East 21st Street, New York, NY 10010

First Edition

Library of Congress Cataloging-in-Publication Data
Names: Heing, Bridey, author.
Title: Marijuana abuse / Bridey Heing.
Description: New York : Rosen Publishing, 2019. | Series: Overcoming addiction | Includes bibliographical references and index. | Audience: Grades 7–12.
Identifiers: LCCN 2017053562| ISBN 9781508179443 (library bound) | ISBN 9781508179603 (pbk.)
Subjects: LCSH: Marijuana abuse—Juvenile literature. | Marijuana abuse—Treatment—Juvenile literature.
Classification: LCC HV5822.M3 H45 2019 | DDC 362.29/5—dc23
LC record available at https://lccn.loc.gov/2017053562

Manufactured in the United States of America

CONTENTS

INTRODUCTION

Drug abuse is generally a complex issue. But marijuana abuse is perhaps even more complex, partly because of the rapid legalization of the drug that is taking place across the United States. At the same time, the use of synthetic marijuana has spread in cities and vulnerable populations across the country, sharing a name but little else with marijuana as we know it. For both of these drugs, treatment is limited—and in the case of synthetic marijuana, barely understood.

Natural marijuana has a long history of use, but the drug's public prominence grew in the twentieth century when propaganda linked it to violent and dangerous behavior. That image eventually gave way to widespread usage, and today the drug is known for having medical benefits and is legal in some states for recreational use. Although the long-term impact of prolonged use is still being studied, natural marijuana is not believed to be addictive in the way other narcotics are, including alcohol or cigarettes, and millions of adults around the world use it without serious side effects. There are many, however, who abuse the drug even where it is legal, and its psychoactive side effects can have serious impact on memory, relationships, and the ability to hold a career.

Synthetic marijuana is a human-made chemical drug that was invented to mimic the active ingredient in natural marijuana, called tetrahydrocannabinol (THC). But while natural marijuana has a fairly predictable response that lasts for a few hours, synthetic marijuana is unpredictable and is linked to self-harm and aggression. Synthetic marijuana is an umbrella term that can refer to any number of synthetic drugs, all of which are made from ever-changing sets of compounds that

Natural marijuana is a plant-derived drug that impacts cognitive abilities, memory, and appetite. It has been legalized for medical and recreational use in jurisdictions around the United States.

are designed to evade regulation and ensure a fast, intense high for users. Because government regulations struggle to keep up with the changing composition of synthetic marijuana products, they can often be sold legally in shops, creating the illusion that they are safe alternatives to marijuana when they are actually far more dangerous.

Treatment for both marijuana and synthetic marijuana abuse is limited to therapies that are designed to help manage behavior, and no medications are recognized by the government as being effective in treatment. Comorbidity, or the emergence of simultaneous addictions or mental health issues, is a serious concern in marijuana and synthetic marijuana abuse. This can exacerbate physical or mental side effects and make it difficult to understand the relationship between cause and symptom. This is particularly true in synthetic marijuana, which is often made of unknown chemicals that can react dangerously with other drugs in a user's system.

The changing nature of marijuana use highlights some of the issues surrounding legality and abuse. Although marijuana is becoming legal in many states and synthetic marijuana is technically legal in many places, both of these drugs can be abused and cause significant lifelong issues for users.

CHAPTER 1

MARIJUANA VERSUS SYNTHETIC MARIJUANA

Marijuana, or cannabis, is one of the most heavily used drugs in the United States and Canada and one that has been the center of the drug control debate for decades. But while natural marijuana has been largely normalized in American society, synthetic marijuana has made the debate surrounding these drugs far more complex. The two groups of drugs, although sharing a name, are actually very different—with unique effects, dangers, and even chemical makeups. Where natural marijuana has come to be associated with medical benefits and potentially safe recreational use among adults, synthetic marijuana is a highly potent and potentially deadly group of drugs that exist at the periphery of the illegal drug market.

Synthetic marijuana is made from an ever-changing set of chemicals and goes by many names. Authorities have struggled to crack down on it because of these changes.

NATURAL MARIJUANA

Natural marijuana is a plant. Its flowers or buds and leaves are dried and its oils can be extracted in order to be smoked. Dried marijuana can also be cooked into foods, most often baked goods like brownies or cookies, although also candies like caramel. The plant requires very specific conditions to grow and comes in many varietals. All marijuana strains have a slightly different effect on the body and mind and are sold by both legal and illegal drug dealers.

The active ingredients that create the psychoactive effect for which marijuana is known are called cannabinoids, and natural marijuana is known as a phytocannabinoid. There are around sixty-five cannabinoids in natural marijuana, but the primary and most potent is tetrahydrocannabinol, or THC. Cannabinoids impact the body and mind in different ways, but most commonly the side effects include dry mouth and increased hunger alongside relaxation and an easing of anxiety. But in some users, marijuana can have the opposite effect, creating paranoia and higher anxiety. These effects can start within a few minutes of taking the drug and usually last a few hours, although side effects including confusion can last for up to a day.

Natural marijuana is not considered physically addictive, and there are no serious or significant withdrawal symptoms associated with stopping use. But the drug's psychological effects, including decreases in anxiety, can cause dependence that can lead to higher levels of stress or panic attacks when regular users transition away from marijuana.

Natural marijuana is also a source of hemp, a low-THC strain, known as a sativa, which can be made into a variety of products. Industrial uses, including creating construction materials and clothing as well as food products and skin care, have been popular around the world for thousands of years. Today, these industries are carefully regulated in the United States to ensure the products cannot be abused as a drug. As we'll learn in later chapters, natural marijuana and THC products, as well as cannabinoid products without THC, are being investigated and legalized because of possible medical benefits, as well.

SYNTHETIC MARIJUANA

While the effects of natural marijuana are understood to be limited, synthetic marijuana poses very real and significant dangers. It is important to note that synthetic marijuana is not made from anything found in natural marijuana. This group of drugs is human-made from an ever-changing set of chemicals and compounds, all of which are designed to interact with the brain in the same way cannabinoids do. But while marijuana users experience often mild side effects, synthetic marijuana

In some places, synthetic marijuana can be sold in stores because it is not technically an illegal drug, despite the extreme effects it can have on the mind and body.

creates extreme and unpredictable results. These drugs are also often sold legally, because of the way in which the United States classes illegal substances, creating an illusion of safety that can be extremely harmful.

Synthetic marijuana products are created as a liquid, which can be vaporized or sprayed onto plant matter to be smoked. These drugs are all made in laboratories based on ever-changing formulas, making them difficult to regulate. Although in recent years the US government has banned some of the chemicals that are known to go into these drugs, others remain legal. As a result, some stores are able to sell these products legally. The drugs themselves go by many names. Two of the most common are Spice or K2, but according to the National Institute on Drug Abuse, names like Joker or Kronic are also in use.

While natural marijuana is known for creating a relaxed state of mind, synthetic marijuana can do the opposite. It can create hallucinations or psychosis, as well as extreme confusion and impaired cognitive functions, including to vision. Violence and suicidal thoughts are also common among users. Like other synthetic drugs, the results of use are highly unpredictable. Since the formula for these drugs is constantly changing, even long-time users can receive a dose that can cause negative reactions or that is of a higher potency than their bodies can handle.

One of the main issues with synthetic marijuana is an issue of branding. Dealers and manufacturers label their drugs as similar to marijuana and even as a legal alternative in areas where marijuana has not been legalized. But these drugs are not an alternative to marijuana—in fact, they share almost nothing in common with natural marijuana and can be life-threatening. Unlike natural marijuana, synthetic marijuana is addictive and has serious withdrawal symptoms. There is also no known treatment because of the relatively new nature of this group of drugs. The affordability of these drugs, along with the perception of them as an alternative to marijuana, has led to epidemic levels of use in cities.

RATES OF USE IN THE UNITED STATES

Marijuana usage in the United States is widespread among both men and women, although statistically men use more heavily than women. In 2016, a Gallup study found that around one in eight American adults use marijuana, or about 13 percent. That's a 6 percent increase since 2013. The percentage of adults who have tried the drug at least once was found to be around 43 percent, compared to just 4 percent in 1969. This is a reflection of both the continued normalization of marijuana throughout the twentieth century and the increasing legalization efforts that have made the drug more accessible through legal channels in recent years.

By comparison, synthetic marijuana rates are relatively low compared to other drugs. But those low rates obscure the drug's significant and increasing damage to communities and especially to teenagers. In 2011, 11 percent of high school seniors had used a synthetic marijuana product. One of the approximately eleven thousand trips to the emergency room was caused by synthetic marijuana, and 75 percent of those admitted were between the ages of twelve and twenty-nine. By 2016, the number of high school seniors who had used synthetic marijuana dropped to 3.5 percent, but teen users are still among the most at risk for overdose or death. In the first half of 2015, the Centers for Disease Control and Prevention (CDC) reported fifteen deaths across forty-eight poison centers in the United States. This is another sharp difference between natural and synthetic marijuana; although synthetic marijuana products can be overdosed on, natural marijuana cannot.

K2 IN DC: A PUBLIC HEALTH CRISIS

Washington, DC, has a long and complex relationship with drug abuse. Once the city with the highest per capita murder rate in the United States, the US capital still struggles with high economic inequality and homelessness. Synthetic drugs like PCP and K2 have spread rapidly among the homeless community, leading to overdoses, deaths, and

(continued on the next page)

The police in Washington, DC, struggle to deal with the often violent and unpredictable behavior of synthetic drug users, despite the public attention to the problem and resources devoted to it.

(continued from the previous page)

public altercations with the authorities. The rise in overdose rates has been swift; between May and June 2014, the number of people admitted to hospitals each month for overdoses rose from 50 to 439. Between 2013 and 2015, all major Drug Enforcement Administration (DEA) operations related to synthetic drugs were carried out in DC, including a seizure of more than fifty tons of the drugs. But outside of those raids, the city has struggled to respond effectively to a crisis that has hit the homeless population, including youths and adolescents. In 2013, the city categorized synthetic marijuana as Schedule 1, a class of drug that receives a more strict police response than others. But the rule lapsed, and the city has struggled to overcome its own limitations in regard to resources. That coupled with the constantly changing nature of synthetics illustrates how even a city that is willing to crack down on synthetic marijuana abuse struggles to do so.

SAME NAME, DIFFERENT IMPACTS

Although sharing a name, natural and synthetic marijuana could not be more different. The two drugs are both psychoactive, but that is where the similarities end. Natural marijuana, though still unsafe for use among those under the legal age where the drug is legalized and illegal in large parts of the country, has a largely predictable and short-lasting set of side effects that are not believed to have a significant or long-lasting impact on the brain. Synthetic marijuana, however, is unpredictable because of its unknown chemical makeup and the ease with which dealers can sell their products using false branding. Synthetic marijuana can create psychosis in users, as well as hallucinations, vomiting, and violence toward others or themselves.

Natural marijuana has been used by humans for millennia, and as a result, our understanding of the drug has evolved quickly since it entered mainstream usage in the mid-twentieth century. But synthetic marijuana is still very new, having only emerged in the early 2000s. Because of the rapid changes and lack of uniformity in synthetic marijuana products, science has struggled to understand how to treat overdose and addiction, even as natural marijuana is being legalized across the country.

CHAPTER 2

A HISTORY OF MARIJUANA ABUSE

Our understanding and use of marijuana has evolved quickly in the past five decades, but the drug has been in use by civilizations around the globe for millennia. Although the term "marijuana" is relatively new, only coming into widespread use in the United States and Canada in the twentieth century, cannabis has been a medicinal and spiritual drug for much of human history. But that started to change in the twentieth century, when its spread in the United States led to the drug being outlawed. This didn't stop its popularity from growing, however; over the course of the twentieth century and into the twenty-first century, marijuana became one of the most widely used illicit drugs in North America. This has led to the decriminalization and even legalization of recreational or medical marijuana use

The use of marijuana has long been linked to religious rituals, going back millennia in cultures around the world.

in many states and cities—and to a complex patchwork of laws and regulation.

MARIJUANA IN THE ANCIENT WORLD

Like other natural drugs, marijuana has a long history dating back thousands of years. It is believed that the drug originated in East Asia, partly because of evidence of ritualized use found in Chinese tombs and records of the drug being used to ease pain as early as 4000 BCE. Archaeologists have found evidence of marijuana use in prehistoric times, including burnt marijuana seeds in Siberia that are dated to around 3000 BCE. Through trade and conquest, the drug spread west through the Indian subcontinent and east to the Korean peninsula, and by 1200 BCE it had made it to the British Isles, throughout Europe, and into Russia.

Marijuana was used as medicine and in religious rituals in the ancient world. The Assyrians called it *qunuba*, referencing the process of smoking it. It was used to ease pain in many cultures, and different religions used it for the psychoactive effects of the drug, which are often associated with spiritual experience. But hemp, the fabric made from the stalks of marijuana plants, has also been used for millennia because of its durability. These uses mirror some of the reasons the drug has been legalized in more recent decades, including for the production of hemp products ranging from clothing to food.

The rapid spread of marijuana eventually brought it to Africa in the first millennia of the Common Era and to South America in the eighteenth and nineteenth centuries. It then spread north to the United States in the early twentieth century, where it quickly became controversial.

MARIJUANA AND THE WEST

Marijuana is not indigenous to the West, but it did reach Europe and Great Britain before the beginning of the Common Era. Even so, the drug's perception in the West has changed significantly over time, and in the nineteenth century, it became associated with other drugs that were in use in the East. As a result, marijuana was thought of as similar to more extreme drugs like opium. This belief was reflected in twentieth-century legislation.

Although marijuana was used in Great Britain for centuries, in the mid-nineteenth century, explorers and anthropologists renewed interest in the drug when they wrote reports on its usage in both Asia and Mexico. William Brooke O'Shaughnessy, an Irish physician, reported on the use of marijuana as medicine in India in 1842 and became a pioneer of medical marijuana research in the West. In 1892, however, another researcher named John Gregory Bourke reported on the use of the drug in Mexico in a more negative light. Although he noted how the drug was used to treat conditions like asthma, he also linked herbal marijuana to hashish, a concentrated cannabis resin that was at that time associated with the bohemian movement. Bourke called hashish a "curse of the East" that led to violent behavior and madness in users—a declaration that was based on fear rather than evidence.

This supposed link between marijuana and violence became the bedrock of how public perception of the drug shifted around the turn of the century. Reports of violent marijuana users began to proliferate, and the public became concerned about the risk marijuana users posed to public safety. Links between marijuana usage and madness spread quickly, particularly in the United

In the twentieth century, propaganda linked marijuana to crime, creating a popular image of the drug as highly dangerous.

States, where the drug was still relatively new. This perception of marijuana largely defined the regulation of the drug over the course of the twentieth century and has left us with potent myths about the drug's impact.

MARIJUANA IN THE UNITED STATES

Marijuana came to the United States with European colonization, and it was first grown as an agricultural product for the cultivation of hemp. In fact, in 1619, the Virginia Assembly passed a law requiring farmers to grow the plant in order to supply the shipping industry with materials. Hemp production was a key agricultural industry in the South until after the Civil War, at which point international imports and other goods replaced hemp.

In the late 1800s, marijuana was a popular ingredient in "patent medicines," which were medical products made by nondoctors and sold around the country despite having little or no proven medical benefit. Marijuana itself was also sold at pharmacies, because at the time it was not illegal. But fears about the drug's impact on the mind started to spread, and by the early 1900s, the drug was the subject of frantic debate. The drug became associated with Mexican immigrants, and fears of this wave of migration resulted in marijuana being represented as a significant danger being brought across the border. In 1905, the *Los Angeles Times* published an exposé on the drug titled "Delirium or Death: Terrible Effects Produced by Certain Plants and Weeds Grown in Mexico" that read in part:

> **Not long ago a man who had smoken a marihuana cigarette attacked and killed a policeman and badly wounded three others; six policemen were needed to disarm him**

PLANTS USEFUL IN DOMESTIC.

d

Marijuana was not illegal until the twentieth century. Prior to that, it was used for medicinal benefits or as part of religious rituals.

and march him to the police station where he had to be put into a straight jacket. Such occurrences are frequent. People who smoke marihuana finally lose their mind and never recover it, but their brains dry up and they die, most of times suddenly.

Increasingly, marijuana became associated with marginalized or impoverished groups, including people of color and artists. Authorities stoked fears by spreading rumors about violent drug users who were trying to get young children addicted to marijuana, and headlines like "Deadly Marijuana Dope Plant Ready for Harvest That Means Enslavement of California Children" were prevalent. The public outcry led to regulation. By 1934, twenty-nine states had laws banning the sale of marijuana, and in 1937, the Marijuana Tax Act was passed by Congress, effectively banning possession of the drug. In 1952, the Boggs Act mandated that marijuana convictions carry the same mandatory minimum sentences as heroin convictions, with a first-time conviction carrying a sentence of at least two years in prison.

HARRY J. ANSLINGER

Harry J. Anslinger is one of the most important people in the history of US drug policy, particularly marijuana regulation. Born in 1892, Anslinger had a military career that took him around the world before returning to the United States in 1929 to work at the Treasury Department's Bureau of Prohibition. Just one year later he founded he Federal Bureau of Narcotics, where he shaped drug policy for three decades. Anslinger was a supporter of full prohibition and criminalization of all drugs, including marijuana. Along with Federal Bureau of Investigation (FBI) director J. Edgar Hoover, Anslinger kept files on celebrities and politicians he believed were using marijuana and other drugs. Anslinger was also active in spreading fear about marijuana, including launching a public service campaign in the 1930s, which proclaimed:

Harry J. Anslinger helped shape and guide US drug policy, including the use of propaganda to shape public perception of drugs like marijuana.

By the tons it is coming into this country—the deadly, dreadful poison that racks and tears not only the body, but the very heart and soul of every human being who once becomes a slave to it in any of its cruel and devastating forms ... Marihuana is a short cut to the insane asylum. Smoke marihuana cigarettes for a month and what was once your brain will be nothing but a storehouse of horrid specters. Hasheesh makes a murderer who kills for the love of killing out of the mildest mannered man who ever laughed at the idea that any habit could ever get him.

Anslinger's influence, and the information he spread about marijuana, is still with us today.

Despite this harsh regulation, marijuana continued to grow in popularity in the second half of the twentieth century. It remained popular with musicians, artists, and writers, fueling the growing counterculture movement in the 1950s and 1960s alongside other psychoactive drugs. In the 1970s, marijuana was becoming normalized to the point that President Richard Nixon passed legislation differentiating it from other drugs, and some decriminalization began for small amounts of the drug. Full legalization was a subject of debate in the public sphere, but it didn't come to much; in the 1980s, the war on drugs brought a temporary end to talk about legalizing marijuana.

President Ronald Reagan's war on drugs was born out of public outcry over teenage drug use and what was seen as out-of-control urban crime rates fueled in part by the spread of hard narcotics like cocaine and heroin. The initiative included multiple laws that made selling or buying marijuana a serious federal crime, and the federal government once again put forward an image of marijuana as a threat to young people and public safety. State laws became similarly strict, and ad campaigns aimed at discouraging young people from beginning to use marijuana proliferated through the 1990s, as did the Drug Abuse Resistance Education (D.A.R.E.) program in public schools.

Marijuana has long been linked to race, associated with the African American community and Mexican immigration. As a result, harsher penalties for marijuana offenses have led to higher rates of incarceration in the black and Latino communities. This has made the war on drugs heavily debated, as many believe it unfairly targeted people of color. This debate has become particularly relevant in recent years as the spread of legalized marijuana has allowed many people to profit from the sale of a drug that has landed people in prison with life sentences, most of whom are still serving time.

MARIJUANA IN POP CULTURE

Marijuana has always been linked to creative communities, from the bohemian movements of the nineteenth century to the Beat Generation of the 1950s. As a result, it has been a shaping influence in our popular culture and appears frequently in both positive and negative portrayals

One of the earliest was the 1936 film *Reefer Madness*, a propaganda film about a group of teenagers who go insane after using marijuana, sometimes called "reefer." The film is a cult classic because of its extreme storyline, but it was far from the last film to portray marijuana as a driving force. Movies like *Cheech and Chong Up In Smoke*, *Half Baked*, *Friday*, and *Pineapple Express* are all reflections of the role of marijuana in society, often depicting regular marijuana users struggling with confusion and disorientation as they deal with a serious problem or life issues. But far from the fear invoked by *Reefer Madness*, these films all rely on marijuana for humor, a sign of changing public perception of the drug.

Movies that took a comedic approach to marijuana thrived in the latter half of the twentieth century as use of the drug became more common.

MARIJUANA TODAY

The war on drugs in the 1980s and 1990s gave way to today's somewhat confusing marijuana policy. The wave of legalization began in the late 1990s, with the 1996 legalization of medical marijuana in California. By 2009, thirteen other states had joined California in granting licenses to patients who receive a prescription for marijuana from a doctor, with which they can then buy marijuana from a regulated dispensary. That same year, the Obama administration announced that federal law enforcement would respect state law and not prosecute legal users who adhered to state laws regarding the medical use of marijuana, which can include easing anxiety or chronic pain, among other uses. As of 2017, twenty-nine states had legalized medical marijuana.

Following the legalization of medical marijuana in many states, cities and other jurisdictions began decriminalizing the possession of small amounts of marijuana. In 2012, Colorado became the first state to legalize the drug for recreational use, and by 2017, eight states and the District of Columbia had followed suit. But the drug is still considered a Schedule 1 illicit substance by the federal government, and this patchwork of different regulations has created a complex system in which what is legal in one state is illegal once one crosses the border. Eric Schlosser captured the confusion caused by these changing drug laws in 1994 when he wrote for the *Atlantic*:

> **In New York state possessing slightly less than an ounce of marijuana brings a $100 fine, rarely collected. In Nevada possessing any amount of marijuana is a felony. In Montana selling a pound of marijuana, first offense, could lead to a life sentence, whereas in New Mexico selling 10,000 pounds of marijuana, first offense, could be punished with a prison term of no more than three years.**

Although used throughout human history, it is in the past century that marijuana has become a controversial and illicit substance. From the use of marijuana as medicine in the early twentieth century to midcentury fears of the drug's possible damage to the mind, marijuana has generated heated debate in society. Today, debates about legalizing marijuana are taking place around the country, despite some states still having strict regulations on the sale and use of the drug. Although it is accepted that use should be restricted to those of legal age, the drug's many medical benefits have prompted a renewed interest in ways that marijuana can be used to help people, and the widespread scientific consensus that the drug does not post significant long-term health side effects has given rise to conversations about the recreational use of the drug.

CHAPTER 3

SYNTHETIC MARIJUANA IN THE TWENTY-FIRST CENTURY

Natural marijuana is an ancient drug, used by humans for centuries, even though perception of the drug has changed significantly in the past one hundred years. But synthetic marijuana doesn't share that history; in fact, the drugs that fall under that broad umbrella only emerged in the United States and Canada in the early 2000s, making them just over a decade old. Despite being relatively new, synthetic marijuana spread quickly and has created a public health crisis to which law enforcement has struggled to respond. Scientists and experts are still trying to understand how best to combat these dangerous compounds, and as a result, abuse has gone largely unchecked.

K2 is one of the most common names for synthetic marijuana, which is sometimes falsely labeled as potpourri.

SCIENTIFIC BREAKTHROUGH TURNED STREET DRUG

The birth of synthetic marijuana can be traced back to 1995, when chemist John Huffman led researchers in creating the first chemical to replicate the brain's response to THC. Called

31

JWH-018, it was part of a study that sought chemical treatments that would mimic marijuana. Huffman did little more with the compound than write a report and publish it, but his findings made the foundation of today's synthetic marijuana market.

According to Huffman, the process of making the compound he discovered is fairly easy. "The chemistry to make these things is very simple and very old," Huffman told the *Washington Post* in 2015. "You only have three starting materials and only two steps. In a few days, you could make 25 grams, which could be enough to make havoc."

Scientist John Huffman discovered the primary chemicals used to make synthetic THC by accident, and manufacturers have used his discovery to create high-potency drugs.

Almost ten years after Huffman's discovery, synthetic marijuana manufacturing began. It first appeared in London in 2004 and spread to the United States by 2008. Within that four-year period, many brands started to create synthetic marijuana, which in some cases can still be sold legally as "potpourri." K2 and Spice are two of the most commonly known names for the drug, while other synthetics made to mimic drugs like crystal meth or LSD also became prevalent around this time.

A PUBLIC HEALTH CRISIS

Use of synthetic marijuana is relatively low compared to other drugs, and in recent years usage has dropped steadily. But usage remains significant among vulnerable populations, including those struggling with homelessness or mental health issues, and among teenagers. In 2011, just a few years after the drug first made it to the United States, around 11 percent of teenagers had tried it, and many young users end up in the hospital every year because of overdose.

The rapid spread of synthetic marijuana can be attributed to a few different things, but most of them fall under marketing. US drug laws are based on the chemical makeup of substances, meaning that regulation is very specific in terms of what is and is not illegal. Synthetic marijuana was and is made of compounds that aren't illegal; as soon as the DEA bans one compound, drug dealers begin producing synthetic marijuana from other compounds that are still technically legal. This allows the drug to be sold in shops across the country as a legal alternative to marijuana, which was and still is illegal as a recreational drug in many places. Some of the brands even call themselves natural, a totally false statement.

Being sold in stores lends synthetic drugs of all kinds an element of legitimacy, and the drugs are marketed as new, exciting, and even safe. The drugs are also often very cheap, being sold for a few dollars with very little oversight. This is one of the reasons the drugs are so heavily used by those who struggle with homelessness or mental health issues, as well as other addictions—synthetic marijuana is accessible and cheap and gives a fast and intense high.

Drugs like K2 and Spice are extremely unpredictable and can be extremely dangerous. Users often swing between wild extremes, going from lethargic to violent at a moment's notice. Agitation and violence, including self-harm and suicide, are common with synthetic drugs, as well as hallucinations and seizures. Irregular and dangerous behaviors are also common. Physical responses like increased heart rate or blood pressure can be exacerbated by combinations of drugs, which can lead to overdose or hospitalization. Since the compounds that make up the drugs are always changing, including from batch to batch, it can be difficult for users to know what they are taking at any one time, which can also create extreme reactions or physical responses that put them in even greater danger.

TACKLING AN EVER-CHANGING PROBLEM

The relatively new nature of synthetic marijuana means that it is little understood by the scientific community, and the drug's constantly changing nature has made it difficult for law enforcement to respond appropriately. Public safety campaigns have made a dent in usage, but because the drugs are in heavy use in vulnerable populations, it can difficult to treat them properly. Concurrent issues like drug addiction and mental health

One difficulty of tackling the use of synthetic marijuana is that as the DEA bans compounds in the drugs, manufacturers create new ones.

concerns are particular challenges, and managing addiction is often secondary to ensuring that the basic needs of individuals are met. As a result, the use of K2 and Spice continues among these populations.

Meanwhile, regulation struggles to keep up. The DEA bans compounds as they discover them, but manufacturers are able to stay one step ahead by changing the compounds they use. At the same time, they use sneaky marketing to ensure their product can be sold in stores, such as labeling it "Not For Human

Consumption" even as they market it as a safe alternative to other drugs.

As is the case with other synthetic drugs, the largest obstacle in effectively combating the use of synthetic marijuana is how much is unknown. The long-term effects of use are still poorly understood, in part because of lack of research and because the compounds themselves are constantly changing. It is also unknown how best to provide treatment, a problem exacerbated by the often simultaneous issues of addiction and other serious threats that come with use of these drugs.

New York City's assistant deputy commissioner for civil enforcement explained to the *New York Times* what makes these unknowns so dangerous: "The users of K2 are literally playing Russian roulette with their bodies. They have no idea what chemicals are in that package or at what concentration."

MYTHS AND FACTS

There are many myths and misunderstandings about marijuana and synthetic marijuana, many of which are based on propaganda—be it good or bad. Here are a few:

MYTH: Synthetic marijuana is a safe alternative to marijuana.

FACT: Although they share a name, synthetic marijuana has nearly nothing in common with natural marijuana and is not safe. In fact, it is often more dangerous than natural marijuana and is far less predictable.

MYTH: Since marijuana is natural, it's safe.

FACT: Marijuana greatly impacts brain functioning, which can put the user in danger. Although some states have ruled that it is safe in controlled environments for adults, it is not safe for those under the legal age and should not be taken before driving or engaging in other activities that require close attention.

MYTH: Synthetic marijuana is always made of the same compounds.

FACT: The makeup of synthetic marijuana changes frequently, and even between batches, so a user has no way of knowing what he or she is ingesting.

CHAPTER 4

TREATMENT FOR MARIJUANA ABUSE

Marijuana abuse and synthetic marijuana abuse are two very different issues with one commonality: treatment is largely limited. While natural marijuana abuse tends to be rooted in dependency rather than addiction, synthetic marijuana is highly addictive and often interconnected with other forms of addictions or mental health issues.

Natural marijuana use is high among almost all categories of Americans, including adolescents. But synthetic marijuana usage is higher among vulnerable groups, including the homeless, and with teens and young adults.

LONG-TERM IMPACTS

The long-term impact of marijuana usage is heavily debated, and often the public debate is based on anecdotal evidence. Research

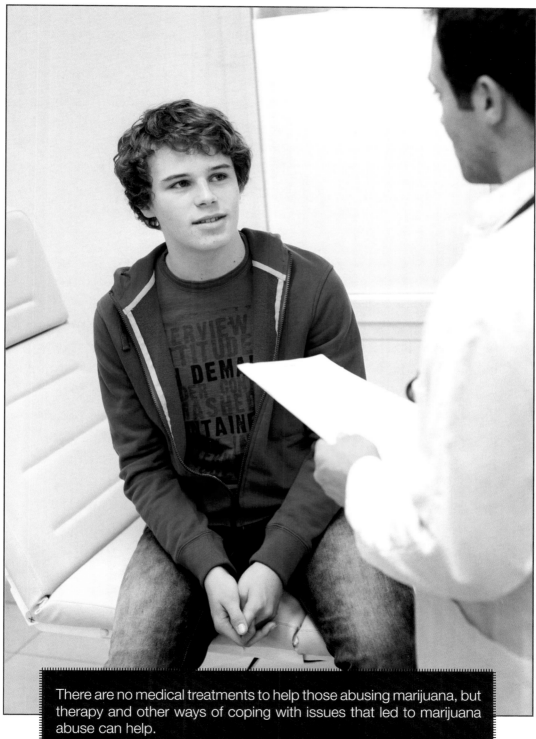

There are no medical treatments to help those abusing marijuana, but therapy and other ways of coping with issues that led to marijuana abuse can help.

has shown that while the drug does not make people become violent or lose sanity, as was once the common perception, it can have an impact on development. Studies have found that heavy marijuana use during adolescence may diminish memory function, making it difficult to learn. Some studies have found similar links in adult users, but the ability of the brain to recover from significant marijuana use is based largely on age; those who take the drug at a younger age may be impacted for a much longer time. This is because the brain is still developing at younger ages, and thus any impact marijuana has can be more permanent.

But according to the National Institute on Drug Abuse, past studies also included users who abused multiple drugs, which makes causation difficult to determine. For that reason, the National Institutes of Health is carrying out a decade-long study called the Adolescent Brain Cognitive Development Study that will work to establish the impact marijuana use has on young and developing brains.

The long-term impact of prolonged synthetic marijuana use is also little understood, partly because of the newness of the drugs. But studies have shown a connection between severe synthetic marijuana use and organ failure or damage, including kidney or renal failure. A study by the National Institutes of Health also found that it could be responsible for reduced brain volume.

TREATMENT FOR MARIJUANA ABUSE

Because natural marijuana is not considered addictive in the same way other drugs are, treatment tends to be based more on behavior therapy. Comorbidity, or the presence of other addictions or mental health issues, tends to be present in

THE ADOLESCENT BRAIN COGNITIVE DEVELOPMENT STUDY

One of the greatest unknowns in relation to marijuana is how the drug impacts young people's brains in the long term. Despite the drug being popular among young people for decades, serious research into how marijuana impacts development and cognition into adulthood is very limited. This is why the Adolescent Brain Cognitive Development Study is so important. Funded by the National Institutes of Health, the study will involve ten thousand children aged nine to ten and will follow them through early adulthood to determine how factors in their childhood and teen years impact their development. The study is not focused solely on marijuana use, but marijuana use will be one of the factors examined. This will help researchers and lawmakers understand the risks marijuana poses to young users and how best to combat those dangers effectively.

those who seek treatment for marijuana abuse, also known as marijuana use disorder. Treatment of those other issues has been found to reduce use of marijuana, indicating that the drug is used as a way to mitigate other issues, rather than being a cause of issues itself. There are no medications approved by the US government as treatment for marijuana abuse, although studies have indicated that sleep aids can help ease users off the drug, as insomnia or other sleep issues tend to occur when the drug is no longer used.

Behavioral therapies that have shown promise as treatment for marijuana abuse vary, but all are centered less on addiction than on changing the behaviors that lead to prolonged marijuana abuse. Cognitive-behavioral therapy, contingency management, and motivational enhancement therapy are all based on finding ways to enhance self-control in order to address underlying issues and provide rewards for not engaging in dangerous or harmful behavior.

Once marijuana users have chosen to stop using the drug, one of the most important steps in maintaining sobriety is giving them the necessary tools to ensure they can avoid relapse. This includes ways to maintain boundaries within friendships if those friends are associated with marijuana use, handle stressful situations in which marijuana was used, and in extreme cases, ensure the user is able to move forward in his or her relationships, career, or education. This underlines the risk of marijuana dependency; although some states have ruled that the drug can be used recreationally, it still has an impact on the way users function, and that impact can be extremely negative. If used too frequently, it can impact the user's ability to learn, form healthy relationships, or progress toward goals. This is particularly risky for young people, who can struggle for the rest of their lives because of the ramifications of heavy marijuana use when they should have been focusing on school and building a career.

While natural marijuana is a risk for developing dependency, synthetic marijuana has been shown to be addictive in a more traditional sense. Withdrawal symptoms such as nausea and seizures have been reported among those who try to go off the drugs, and cravings for synthetic marijuana are extremely strong, so breaking the addiction is all the more difficult. For synthetic marijuana, effective treatment is still being developed. As with natural marijuana, comorbidity is a significant issue in targeting treatment and establishing baseline causes for physical and mental issues. But it is unclear if behavioral treatments are as effective for synthetic marijuana abuse treatment as they are for abuse of natural marijuana, and no medications have been approved by the US government for use as treatment.

Interestingly, some advocates and scientists, including the chemist who discovered the key compound used to create synthetic marijuana, feel that legalizing natural marijuana would help reduce the use of synthetic marijuana. One of the reasons the drug is used, at least in the first instance, is as a way to evade drug tests; synthetic drugs do not turn up in traditional testing, while natural marijuana does. Legalization advocates feel that making natural marijuana legal would undercut the sale of synthetics, which often rely on false labeling that claims the drugs are safe alternatives to illegal marijuana. But this solution would not apply to young people, who would likely be excluded from use of legal marijuana because of age requirements.

ABUSE AND LEGALITY

Although natural marijuana is being legalized around the country, it is important to remember that even drugs that are legal can be abused. Abuse doesn't just apply to illegal drugs; any drug or substance can be abused if it is used in ways that are harmful to the health of the user or to others. This is true of marijuana as well. Use of marijuana can greatly impact one's ability to learn, carry out functions that require attention, or

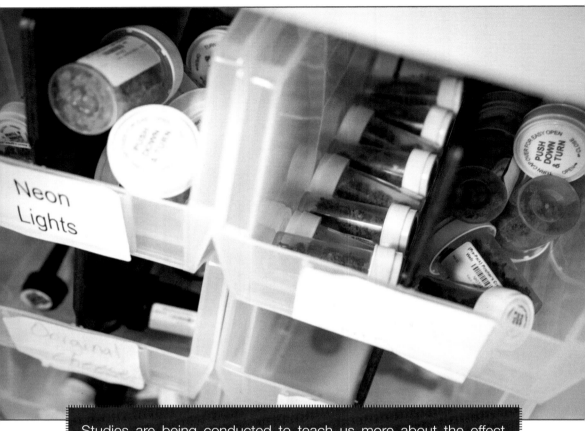

Studies are being conducted to teach us more about the effect marijuana has on developing minds, which could include overall cognitive function.

maintain healthy relationships. For young people, it might even impair long-term cognitive function, although more research is needed to understand potential links between marijuana use and long-term impacts.

SEEKING HELP

If a friend or loved one is struggling with marijuana or synthetic marijuana abuse, it is important to find a trained adult who can

One way to support those who are struggling with marijuana abuse is to help them avoid situations in which they may be tempted to use again.

help them safely stop using. If you feel it is safe, let them know that you are there to support them as they transition away from marijuana use. It is important for former marijuana users to be given tools that will help them navigate situations in which they may feel pressure to use again; supporting them at those times is an important way to keep them from relapsing. Providing them with alternative ways to handle difficult emotions is one way to do this, as is giving them fun things to do that are not related to drug use.

If you feel as if you have become dependent on marijuana and it is affecting your life, you can also reach out for help. Talk to a trusted family member, counselor, or teacher. Although marijuana is not physically addictive, if its use interferes with your life, it can be a problem. Synthetic marijuana, however, is highly dangerous and should immediately be brought up with a health care provider or therapist. The first step to addressing that you want to make a change in your life is reaching out to others for help.

TEN GREAT QUESTIONS
TO ASK A MEDICAL MARIJUANA USER

1. How did you decide to start using medical marijuana?

2. Did you have any concerns before using medical marijuana?

3. How does medical marijuana help you?

4. What is the process of getting a medical marijuana card?

5. Were you given any guidance by your doctor on how to use medical marijuana?

6. What are some of the steps you take to ensure you do not become dependent on it?

7. What do you wish people knew about medical marijuana users?

8. How does medical marijuana differ from recreational marijuana use?

9. What did you think medical marijuana use would be like, and were your assumptions right?

10. What do you feel would make medical marijuana more effective or safer?

CHAPTER 5

THE FUTURE OF MARIJUANA ABUSE

Marijuana and synthetic marijuana are complex drugs moving in opposite directions. While natural marijuana is becoming normalized and legalized, the push to criminalize and combat synthetic marijuana is becoming more and more pronounced. This leaves both of the drugs in a difficult place in terms of understanding what the future holds for treatment and understanding of abuse. Although more research is needed, both natural marijuana and synthetic marijuana are likely to undergo significant changes in years to come that could change the way we think of two very different but linked substances.

LEGALIZATION

Marijuana legalization has been a slow and steady process that has swept across the United States, beginning with medical

The movement for legalization of marijuana is growing. In 2012, Colorado and Washington became the first states to fully legalize marijuana, which includes recreational use.

marijuana and more recently moving toward legalization for recreational use. But with no federal deregulation, the legalization process is left to the states, creating a complex system of differing legislation that can change drastically from one place to another. While one state may have full legalization for adult users, the next state over could impose strict sentences for even first-time convictions.

But polling has shown that more and more Americans favor marijuana legalization in one form or another. In 2013, Americans favored legalization over criminalization for the first time, with 58 percent saying it should be legalized. By comparison, when the question was first posed in 1969, only 12 percent of respondents agreed with legalization. A 2017 Harvard-Harris poll found that 86 percent of those surveyed supported marijuana legalization in some form, including 49 percent favoring full legalization and 37 percent favoring medical marijuana legalization. Those who said it should remain fully illegal made up just 14 percent of respondents.

Many advocacy groups that favor legalizing marijuana point to other drug problems, like the opioid crisis, as being more deserving of attention than marijuana abuse. Others argue that legalization would have a significant effect on the black market drug dealing that funds cartels and other operations that pose a threat to people across borders. But lawmakers and some law enforcement officials have been far from convinced by these arguments, and many efforts to legalize marijuana stalled in 2017.

Questions also remain about how best to regulate the drug, including legal ages at which to allow its use, where and in what amounts it can be held for personal use, and how to ensure sales are properly monitored to ensure compliance. There are also questions surrounding the issue of use in public. In Washington, DC, where the drug was legalized for recreational use, ongoing problems with people smoking in public have sparked a widespread public debate about how to ensure spaces aren't overwhelmed by the smell of marijuana. Like other legal narcotics, such as alcohol and cigarettes, it is important that legalization not be misunderstood as a free hand in use; marijuana, like other drugs, has to be carefully regulated to ensure safe use.

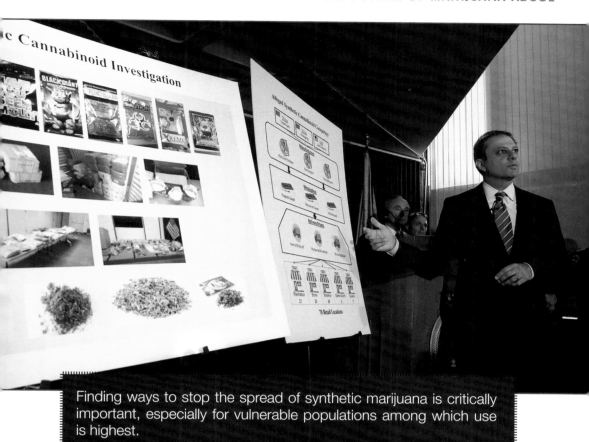

Finding ways to stop the spread of synthetic marijuana is critically important, especially for vulnerable populations among which use is highest.

COMBATING SYNTHETIC MARIJUANA

Even as efforts to legalize natural marijuana are spreading across the country, efforts to combat the use of synthetic marijuana are also becoming more widely debated. These drugs, which are much newer than natural marijuana, are so poorly understood that authorities are struggling to get a handle on the problem. Although marijuana advocates feel that legalizing natural marijuana could help limit interest in these supposed alternatives, it is unclear if there is a connection between legalization and a slowdown in the use of synthetics.

51

Public safety campaigns, particularly aimed at teenagers, have been taken up around the country, and many cities and states are working to ensure charges can be brought against those who sell synthetic marijuana. But with so much unknown—from the compounds that make up the drugs to the long-term impact of abuse—research is needed to understand how to effectively contain and eliminate use of synthetics.

A CONTROVERSIAL DRUG

Marijuana has a long and complicated history, being used continuously from prehistoric times to the present. That history became far more complex in the twentieth century, when the drug became a popular and mainstream substance hounded by myths and rumors. From the early twentieth century, when the drug was associated with violence, to the midcentury fears of teenagers running amok thanks to reefer madness, to today's widespread legalization, the story of marijuana is a story of ever-changing perception and public attitude.

But that attitude has a strange counterpart in synthetic marijuana, a human-made chemical drug that has been falsely marketed as an alternative to marijuana. Sold legally in many places, the drug is unsafe and has extreme side effects, including the violence and hallucinations that were once associated with marijuana abuse. Popular with young people and vulnerable populations, the drug has become a public health crisis that officials are struggling to contain.

These two polar opposites—natural marijuana that is becoming more and more normalized and synthetic marijuana that is a legal but dangerous substance—highlight different issues surrounding addiction and treatment. Both exist at the

The majority of Americans support legalization of marijuana in some form, highlighting the complex history of this ever-evolving drug.

intersection of legality and illegality, but both pose different threats from abuse. Whether legal or not, both marijuana and synthetic marijuana can have a serious impact on the lives of young users, and the ramifications of regular use can be detrimental for years to come.

As research continues into how to treat marijuana abuse, the next ten years could see significant changes in how we understand these drugs and how best to address abuse of both natural and synthetic marijuana. Today's limited understanding could give way to a deeper sense of how to address these issues, which could transform the way we think about both natural marijuana and synthetic marijuana.

GLOSSARY

CANNABINOIDS Compounds that make up the active ingredient in marijuana, causing the side effects for which the drug is known.

COMORBIDITY The presence of one or more health issues, such as addiction and chronic disease or mental health concerns.

HALLUCINATIONS Visions, sounds, or other stimuli that appear to be real to those experiencing them but are actually caused by drugs.

HASHISH A resin made of marijuana, with high potency.

HEMP A fiber made from marijuana plants with low levels of THC.

INDIGENOUS People, flora, or fauna that are native to an area.

MARIJUANA A plant that contains psychoactive compounds that can be smoked in order to create psychoactive side effects.

NARCOTICS Addictive drugs, often illegal, that impact mood and behavior.

PARANOIA Heightened fear and anxiety.

PCP Phencyclidine, also known as PCP, a highly addictive synthetic drug with unpredictable side effects, including hallucinations, increased body temperature, and aggression.

PHYTOCANNABINOID A plant, such as marijuana, that contains cannabinoids.

POTENCY The concentration and strength of a drug, directly related to the drug's side effects.

PSYCHOACTIVE Drugs and other substances that impact the mind and cognitive function.

PSYCHOSIS A mental disorder in which the sufferer loses touch with reality.

RECREATIONAL Use that is for fun rather than medical benefit.

RITUALIZED Use linked to a religious or other ritual.

SCHEDULE 1 In the United States, a category of illicit substances that have no medical benefit or use that could justify any level of legalization, including heroin and cocaine.

STRAINS Types of marijuana, all of which have different levels of THC and other compounds.

SYNTHETIC MARIJUANA A chemical drug made to affect the same parts of the brain as THC, but with highly unpredictable and dangerous side effects.

TETRAHYDROCANNABINOL (THC) The strongest active compound in marijuana.

FOR MORE INFORMATION

Canadian Centre on Substance Use and Addiction (CCSA)
75 Albert Street, Suite 500
Ottawa, ON K1P 5E7
Canada
(613) 235-4048
Website: http://www.ccsa.ca
Twitter: @CCSACanada
This Canadian governmental organization focuses on researching
    drug abuse and addiction.

Centre for Addiction and Mental Health (CAMH)
1001 Queen Street West
Toronto, ON M6J 1H4
Canada
(416) 535-8501
Website: http://www.camh.ca
Email: info@camh.ca
Facebook: @CentreforAddictionandMentalHealth
Twitter: @CAMHnews
The CAMH is a Canadian medical organization that focuses on
    mental health and addiction issues, including research into
    natural and synthetic marijuana abuse and treatment.

Marijuana Policy Project (MPP)
PO Box 77492
Washington, DC 20013
(202) 462-5747

Website: https://mpp.org
Email: info@mpp.org
Facebook: @MarijuanaPolicyProject
Twitter: @MarijuanaPolicy
The MPP is the largest organization in the United States whose
    mission is to end marijuana prohibition.

National Institute on Drug Abuse (NIDA)
Office of Science Policy and Communications
Public Information and Liaison Branch
6001 Executive Boulevard
Room 5213, MSC 9561
Bethesda, MD 20892
(301) 443-1124
Website: https://www.drugabuse.gov
Facebook: @NIDANIH
Twitter: @NIDAnews
This governmental organization publishes reports and information
    about drug abuse, as well as studies into rates of drug use,
    including natural and synethic marijuana.

National Institutes of Health (NIH)
9000 Rockville Pike
Bethesda, MD 20892
(301) 496-4000
Website: https://nih.gov
Email: NIHinfo@od.nih.gov
Facebook: @nih.gov
Twitter: @NIH
The NIH is a governmental organization that researches public
    health and mental health, including addiction.

FOR FURTHER READING

Acred, Carla. *Cannabis Issues*. Cambridge, MA: Independence, 2014.

Allen, John. *Legalizing Marijuana*. San Diego, CA: ReferencePoint Press, 2015.

Benjamin, Daniel. *Marijuana*. New York, NY: Cavendish Square, 2014.

Collins, Anna. *Marijuana: Abuse and Legalization*. New York, NY: Lucent Press, 2017.

Cunningham, Anne. *Critical Perspectives on Legalizing Marijuana*. New York NY: Enslow Publishing, 2016.

Gillard, Arthur. *Medical Marijuana*. New York, NY: Greenhaven Press, 2014.

Goldstein, Margaret. *Legalizing Marijuana: Promises and Pitfalls*. Minneapolis, MN: Lerner Publishing Group, 2016.

Mooney, Carla. *The Dangers of Marijuana*. San Diego, CA: ReferencePoint Press, 2017.

Perritano, John. *Marijuana and Synthetics*. Broomall, PA: Mason Crest, 2017.

Sinatra, Caitlin A., and Selena Dugan-Fields. *Let's Talk About Marijuana*. Albany, OR: Let's Talk Publications, 2015.

BIBLIOGRAPHY

Anderson, Jeffrey. "Spice World." *Washington City Paper*, September 4, 2015. http://www.washingtoncitypaper.com /news/article/13047146/spice-world-synthetic-drugs-have -plagued-dc-for-years-what.

Anslinger, Harry J., and Will Oursler. *The Murderers: The Shocking Story of the Narcotics Gangs*. New York, NY: Farrar, Straus and Cudahy, 1961.

Booth, Martin. *Cannabis: A History*. New York, NY: Picador, 2005.

Martin, Scott C. "A Brief History of Marijuana Law in America." *Time*, April 20, 2016. http://time.com/4298038/marijuana -history-in-america.

McCarthy, Justin. "One in Eight US Adults Say They Smoke Marijuana." Gallup, August 8, 2016. http://news.gallup.com /poll/194195/adults-say-smoke-marijuana.aspx.

McCoy, Terrence. "How This Chemist Unwittingly Helped Spawn the Synthetic Drug Industry." *Washington Post*, August 9, 2015. https://www.washingtonpost.com/local/social-issues /how-a-chemist-unwittingly-helped-spawn-the-synthetic -drug-epidemic/2015/08/09/94454824-3633-11e5-9739 -170df8af8eb9_story.

NIDA. "Synthetic Cannabinoids (K2/Spice)." National Institute on Drug Abuse, April 7, 2016. https://www.drugabuse.gov /drugs-abuse/synthetic-cannabinoids-k2spice.

Nir, Sarah Maslin. "K2 Overdoses Surge in New York: At Least 130 Cases This Week Alone." *New York Times*, July 14, 2016. https://www.nytimes.com/2016/07/15/nyregion /k2-overdose-spike-in-new-york-at-least-130-cases-this -week-alone.html.

Reuters staff. "Deaths from Synthetic Marijuana Use Rise Sharply in US: CDC." Reuters, June 11, 2015. https://www.reuters.com/article/us-marijuana-deaths/deaths-from-synthetic-marijuana-use-rising-sharply-in-u-s-cdc-idUSKBN0OR2EI20150611.

Reuters staff. "Synthetic Marijuana: A Dangerous Drug at a Cheap Price." Centers for Disease Control and Prevention. https://www.cdc.gov/nceh/hsb/synthetic_marijuana.htm.

Romey, Kristin. "Ancient Cannabis 'Burial Shroud' Discovered in Desert Oasis." National Geographic, October 4, 2016. http://news.nationalgeographic.com/2016/10/marijuana-cannabis-pot-weed-burial-shroud-china-ancient-discovery-scythians-turpan-archaeology-botany.

Schlosser, Eric. "Marijuana and the Law." Atlantic, September 1994. https://www.theatlantic.com/magazine/archive/1994/09/marijuana-and-the-law/308958.

Schlosser, Eric. "Reefer Madness." Atlantic, August 1994. https://www.theatlantic.com/magazine/archive/1994/08/reefer-madness/303476.

Sloman, Larry, et al. Reefer Madness: A History of Marijuana. New York, NY: St. Martin's Griffin, 1998.

Thompson, Matt. "The Mysterious History of 'Marijuana.'" Code Switch, NPR, July 22, 2013. http://www.npr.org/sections/codeswitch/2013/07/14/201981025/the-mysterious-history-of-marijuana.

INDEX

ABOUT THE AUTHOR

Bridey Heing is a writer and book critic based in London. She holds degrees in political science and international affairs from Depaul University and Washington University in Saint Louis. She has written about Iranian affairs, women's rights, and art and politics for publications like the *Economist*, Hyperallergic, and the *Times Literary Supplement*. She also writes about literature and film. She enjoys traveling, reading, and exploring museums.

PHOTO CREDITS

Cover Iakov Filimonov/Shutterstock.com; p. 5 Nancy Honey/Cultura /Getty Images; pp. 8, 51 Spencer Platt/Getty Images; pp. 7, 16, 30, 38, 48 OpenRangeStock/Shutterstock.com; p. 10 Sun Sentinel/Tribune News Service/Getty Images; p. 13 Bill Clark/CQ-Roll Call Group /Getty Images; p. 17 Prakash Mathema/AFP/Getty Images; p. 20 David Pollack/Corbis Historical/Getty Images; p. 22 Florilegius/SSPL /Getty Images; p. 24 Bettmann/Getty Images; p. 27 Movie Poster Image Art/Moviepix/Getty Images; p. 31 Wendy Galietta /The Washington Post/Getty Images; p. 32 John Fletcher Jr. /The Washington Post/Getty Images; p. 35 David Butow/Corbis Historical/Getty Images; p. 39 Burger/Canopy/Getty Images; p. 44 Jabin Botsford/The Washington Post/Getty Images; p. 45 martin-dm /E+/Getty Images; p. 49 Joe Raedle/Getty Images; p. 53 Wictor Szymanowicz/Barcroft Media/Getty Images.

Design and Layout: Nicole Russo-Duca; Editor and Photo Researcher: Elizabeth Schmermund